Dance Craze

Dance Craze

Poems by
Antonia Clark

Published by Bellevue Books
2020

ISBN: 978-1-7336142-1-4

For my sweet ol' Tomcat—

Still crazy about you after all these years.

Let's dance!

Acknowledgments

Thanks to the editors of these journals in which many of the poems in this volume were first published:

2River View, Allegro Poetry Magazine, Avatar Review, Better Than Starbucks, Blue Lake Review, Clementine Unbound, Dodging the Rain, Eclectica Magazine, Foliate Oak, Frostwriting, Halfway Down the Stairs, Hanging Moss Journal, Innisfree Poetry Journal, misfitmagazine, Monongahela Review, Red River Review, Rusty Truck, Soundzine, Softblow, Street Light Press, Tipton Poetry Journal, Verse-Virtual, Verse Wisconsin, Wilderness House Literary Review, Word Riot.

"A Brief History of Rain" won first place in the Inter-Board Poetry Community competition in May, 2018, and appears on the IBPC website at webdelsol.com.

Special Thanks

To all the poets and teachers from whom I've learned so much. And to my writing buddies at 77 Sunset Beach, where most of these poems began.

A Note to the Reader

Not all of these poems are autobiographical. But some are. And even in those, I often play fast and loose with the facts. I alter events or stretch the truth in order to tell a larger truth. Some of these poems contain secrets. Some contain lies. But of course, I'll never tell you which are which.

Poems

Rearview

Imagine Me

Dance Craze

Rearview

Family Dynamics: A Brief History

Already a month late,
I send my mother a blizzard
of pain, arrive ten minutes
after she gets to the hospital.

I'm not quite the idea
she's been carrying around
all this time. Dad drinks it in
while Mom sleeps it off.
I'm a storm squall of trouble.
They make the best of it,
boil bottles, diapers,
rubber nipples.

But babies keep appearing
like rabbits out of hats. A trick
that soon stops amusing.
She says he never asks permission.
He says she never gives consent.

She tries vitamins, mineral salts.
He tries camouflage, subterfuge.
She pops barbies and hearts.
He pops cans of Pabst.

I hide the evidence, change
the babies, navigate cross-currents
of duty and desire. One day,
without asking, I'll disappear
from their story. In the next one,
I'll swing my empty arms, wear
a tinkling pop-top necklace, move
to the music of the spheres.

The Fabulous Fifties

We embraced the road,
with no time to rest, farm to town,
city to suburb, east to west.

We got the Fairlane, Thunderbird,
Impala, Bel Air. We got radial
tires, fins, grilles, flair.

We had hot times, leisure time,
country and soul. We all went
to the hop. Got rock and roll.

We got McDonald's, Kleenex,
aluminum cans, styrofoam,
TV dinners, Teflon pans.

We got beatniks and boomers,
and the Big Bang, transistor radios,
Spanky and Our Gang.

We got existential dread
and doubt, Miltown and Marilyn,
kilotons, fallout.

We got DNA, LSD, discovered
our senses, got down, got older,
got truth or consequences.

1957

Mom cried over Bogart,
but wouldn't let us watch Elvis.
Somewhere, Sputnik was beeping.
That winter, we all had the Asiatic flu.

Skippy Sketino killed a rat
on our front porch. In our pajamas,
we knelt in front of the window
and watched him squash it in a corner
with an old sponge mop.

He swung it by the tail, and hurled it
into the woods across the road.
Then we went back to sniffling
and whining. Listening for radio signals
from Martians. Arguing over Monopoly money.

The Russians were on everybody's mind.

Escape Artists

It was an art we practiced daily—
how to scrape by without getting
caught — or scratched too deep.
We slid under the chain-link fence
at the far end of the playground,
scooting butts and backs through a hole
the boys had scooped out beneath it.
No one ever dared to tell,
but it wouldn't have mattered.
We were eager for danger,
for taking chances. Not that we had
a place to go, opportunities waiting.
The point was to get out. We had
our childhoods trapped inside us
and needed to ditch them in a hurry.
On the other side, there was only
a jungle of overgrown brambles,
a path that ended at another fence,
and no way over or under it.
We always had to take the long way back
and come up with a good story.

Deaf Ears

The Blob scared us silly,
left us helpless and shivering.
That and Dirk Dooley
who skulked around our house
at night, peeked through the screen
when we slept on the porch
in our shortie pjs. Dirty Dirk,
who grabbed at our blouses,
tried to see up our skirts.
A boy like that would try anything:
his hot breath on a summer night,
his grubby hand in your Tuesday
underpants, his wet tongue poking.
Our mothers warned us: evil
seeks the heedless, grows
in the dark. They lectured
on the plethora of sows' ears,
the dearth of silk purses,
the perilous paths of sin. How a girl
gone wrong can never get right again.
None of which stopped me
from slipping a stolen lipstick
into my purse, a cigarette in my pocket,
rolling up the waistband of my skirt,
and sashaying off the bus
to seek the error of my ways.

Theology

I've long since parted company
with that sad, triangled god
who monitored the endless hours
of my childhood, the Überparent
who took over when the earthly
ones were busy or couldn't see,
for instance, me in my room

torn between junior sainthood
and less spiritual aspirations, one
minute praying for a vision, the next
studying the *Illustrated History of Art*
trying to make sense of male anatomy.

I'm done with that dour presence
that hovered above the hard winter
ground, where I lay with a neighbor
boy, his fisherman-knit sweater rough
against my chest, we two snug
in the questionable belief that we
could make ourselves invisible.

Today I only pray to minor gods
who've proven themselves good
listeners—ghosts, stones, small
animals. No wish to unravel mysteries,
unveil what's unrevealed, but will
always choose to follow the call
of geese, the river's slow meander,
a line of tracks across an open field.

Substitute Kansas

I don't rule out much, but I could substitute Kansas
for just about anyplace and decide not to go there.

Some places that I actually know about, for instance
the backsides of outbuildings, e.g., toolsheds,

could pop up anywhere—a good thing, since we all
need one now and then to do something out behind.

Where I grew up—in a state mistaken as zipped up,
straitlaced—there were endlessly available erections

of scrap lumber and tin in all the backyards,
thrown together by the dads for seemly purposes,

quickly appropriated by those in urgent need
of cover, and we were all faster learners then.

It's more complicated now. We have to weigh risks,
which slows us down considerably. No more in and out

of the magic sack like rabbits. and Kansas is probably
a lot closer than it appears in the rearview mirror.

Drifter

He had another birthday in Missouri,
then decided to really start living.
He had another beer in Bear Creek,
then lit out for parts even more unknown.
He had another woman in Spokane,
but that was far, far away.
He had another name for himself,
something wild and a little savage,
but he shared it with no one.
He had a long acquaintance with desire,
an intimate knowledge of dread,
a love affair with the road and the night,
a way of turning a woman's head
and any situation to advantage, given
a good listener and a certain kind of light.

Sweet Talk

He was the kind of guy with a story
to tell, a way of spinning sentences
like taffy, one thing after another,
a sticky web of connections a girl
could get lost in. Honey dripped
from his fingers, caramel kisses
from his lips, He knew how to dangle
a come-on like a candy necklace—
cheap sweets on a string.

I was a girl with a fondness for fiction,
eager and willing to suspend disbelief
for a quick lick of the icing spoon,
a promise of cinnamon sizzles,
cherry hearts. In his rented room,
we played a sugar-coated version
of baby, baby, baby. I was the kind
of girl with a constant craving. He was
the kind of guy who knew my kind.

Daredevil

I believed nothing could touch me, the flashing shield
of my yellow dress, the shrine of my bright
white hair, faith like a folded love note
tucked in my pocket.

I put an easy distance between me and my destiny
with red shoes and grit. I stepped off curbs,
fearless, and like the taxis, death
swerved to let me pass.

Like No Tomorrow

I was in a hurry, made short work
of burdens and hurdles,
flinging excuses into the wind.
I was verbal and fertile.
I skipped and skirted and circled.
Put my faith in cut and run.

When the sand shifted
under my feet, I took to the air,
a kind of winged victory
over circumstance and ceremony.

I didn't yet know what the seasons
would have to say. Or boulders,
or mountains. Or how debris
accumulates: dust, bone, shed skin.

Never a thought of roadblocks
dead ends, wilderness. Lies
in the bottom of the glass,
in the chambers of the heart.
The truths of the body.

I was the girl with a thousand faces
hurtling into the future—believing
the present was all that mattered,
for a while even believing
I had nothing to lose.

Breaking and Entering

He broke into my life like a midnight burglar,
picking the locks, rifling drawers,
strewing rooms with the debris of desire.

All I remember now is the long bright scrape
of metal on metal, the heavy tread of insistence,
the way will shatters like glass.

And afterward, smoke and sweat, the cloying
scent of heliotrope, the unbreathable air.

Return to Sender

Once he was a fence, with a prominent Keep Out sign,
and I was the hole the boys peeked through.

Once he was a street with a clear destination
and I was the corner that forced him to turn left.

Once he was a door, unlatched on a windy night.
and I was the rusty hinge that drove everyone crazy.

If he were a package stamped Occupant Unknown,
I'd bribe the mailman to make me his return address.

Out of My Mind

My mind was something I couldn't find
my way out of. A hedge maze, a city
full of one-way streets, a bad dream.

This way, he said. He handed me a ball
of twine, a map marked with arrows,
a small white pill and a glass of warm milk.

In the morning, there was nothing to do
but leave him with his tangle of string
and empty glass. I took the map and ran.

His Lucky Number

He had a heart closed as a fist,
a talent for bad deals, dead ends,
a bank account like an empty bowl.

I was his last chance, his lucky number,
the flash of a silver coin spinning
out of reach in his fading dream.

Fishing on Misery River

Toward morning, we finally left
our sputtering fire to smolder—
no sense in more pretense—and fell
into rough sleep. We two anglers,
casting deep into the murky
heart, sending down questions like hooks,
keen, barbed steel, bright with bloody bait—
all those quick silver fins flashing.

"Fishing on Misery River" and "Driving Home after Drying
Out" are Tonichkas. The Tonichka, a form I invented, is a
poem of 8 lines, with 8 syllables in each. The first letters of
each line spell out Tonichka, a diminutive or endearment
my mother called me when I was very small.

Driving Home after Drying Out

Towns I've never heard of pop up
on exits—Temperance, Dryden.
No one risks a joke. My mother
insists on music—loud AM
country, full of losers, heartache,
hard living. The words, she says, just
kill me. I read the warning signs
ahead: Caution. Slippery When Wet.

Elsewhere

We left Little Rock
in a frenzy, drove all night
to Delirium, Texas
where we came face to face
with our oldest fears.
The trees, all indifferent,
tossed their heads in a dry
wind. The parched ground
cracked underfoot,
begged for our tears.

But we were only passing
through, on our way
elsewhere, to fervor,
derangement, wild unrest.
To sinuous coastlines
snaking up and down
the continent, the ceaseless,
senseless ocean
heaving against the rocks.

House of Cards

Once we argued over details
of construction—

the number of rooms, pitch
of the roof—

forgetting doors until we found
ourselves locked inside.

Too late then to repair shaky stories,
shore up the crumbling foundation.

We shuddered at distant rumbles,
the shrill from the trestle.

Walls wobbled at every tremor,
shivering toward collapse.

Outside, our useless blue bicycles
leaned against the walls.

Tutti's

There was no one I knew at Tutti's but Earl,
still tending bar. And it was the West Side now.
Tutti died three, four years ago, Earl said.
Wife sold the place in a snap, made a bundle.
We watched somebody else's black and white
holiday on TV, then the news break — snow
and sirens — and down the bar, a man asked
no one in particular if this is all it comes down to.

He just shrugged when I asked after Big Lou,
who once played bass with the Ballard Boys.
And no one remembered Sweet Jack Simms,
who sang "Bye Baby Blues" and "Don't Try"
or the girl who'd loved him once, who'd spent
night after night crying on Earl's shoulder.
Whole lot of girls like that, Earl said, slapping
down two bucks change. If they're smart,
they leave this sorry-ass town and don't come back.

Paraphernalia

I miss the head shops—

the tie-dyed sheets, Indian
bedspreads, beaded curtains
swaying in the perfumed breeze—

jasmine, patchouli, rain forest

the pipes, screens, bongs
roach clips, rolling papers,
Jimi and Janis and Pink Floyd

under the black lights

and those sweet, skinny boys
with their ponytails and bandanas,
who really believed the war

was somewhere else

who'd pull you close, tell you
everything's cool, baby,
relax, baby, everything's

gonna be all right.

At the Divide

When we pass through
one another's thoughts,

it's on horseback
or pack mule,
stragglers riding deep
into the canyon,

red walls striated
with layers of sediment,
studded with fossilized
life forms, locked
in stone, indecipherable.

My shadow's length
reminds me not to linger.
I train my eyes straight
ahead and grip the reins,

knees pressed tight
to the heaving sides
of my mount.

Been There

The closet
the woods
the gravel pit—

all for the same reasons.

The driver's seat
the back seat
the hot seat—

with the usual connotations.

The cusp
the lip
the brink
the rim—

paralyzed by doubt.

Hotel room
back room
court room
waiting room—

and no way out.

Rope

Fibrous, scratchy, hanging
in the garage, great loose loops
like a dead woman's braid.

It's known bad company—
the shovel and spade, the slender
branch, the latched wooden box
we keep from the children.

It can float, but briefly. Slowly,
it sinks, uncoils, snakes
through black water, dragging down
light trapped in frayed filaments.

I'd like to ask: What will you do
the next time you find
someone drowning?

Before it existed, we hauled
and carried, we learned
how to hold things together,

learned what to do in any
emergency, used our wits
to survive, our arms
to save one another.

No matter what happens,
it always says, *Trust me—*
Swing out over the pond.

Rearview

As far back as I can see,
there's no one coming, just
a long stretch of Iowa road
unwinding behind me. No trace
of what I'm leaving—a house
I need to believe is full of absence.
We always made love in the dark
in case we needed to pretend
it hadn't happened.

Dry grass and rusted fences
rush by like bad memories.
I have to keep reminding myself
that I'm the one in motion.

This road's so straight, all I can do
is accelerate, watch for a sign,
an exit. Still, from time to time,
I adjust the rearview mirror as if
I might catch sight of you, crazy
with pain and desire and change
of heart, gaining on me.

The Woman Who Picked Me Up

had slammed on the brakes
of her rusty Dodge, deciding
to pull over, after all

had streaked hair and muddy boots,
a lazy eye and, once in a while,
a wistful look

had a gallon of milk and a six-pack,
a torn map, and a hammer
on the seat between us

had to have been under 30, but
claimed she was no spring chicken
in dog years

had her radio tuned to country
and tried to sing along, but didn't
really know the words

had a way of asking questions, then
not waiting for the answers, in a breezy
inoffensive way

had two kids back at her mother's,
one that cried all the time, one
that never did

had just got out of someplace,
I don't know what or where,
but it changed her life

had seen the light, turned
a corner, put the past behind her,
and a four-day drive ahead

had me thinking, when I got clean
I'd buy a pickup, drive hard and fast
to someplace I've never been.

Imagine Me

This Poem Is Concerned

with hiding places,
with corners and holes,
shadows, the slender space
behind the door, the envelope
of dark under the bed.

with bones and stones,
with mineral deposits
and calcification.
with chalk dust, grains
of sand, grit and gristle.

with the body's busyness,
its murmurs and catches,
stridor and wheeze, crackle
and rale and crepitation.

with camouflage, cover-up,
a swath of gauze, hastily
wound to conceal curve
and hollow, the true shape
of its emptiness.

Bareback

We are as horse and rider,
the hours and I. They ever
quickening the pace
as I draw on the reins
playing for time.

Milestones blur by. Dust
blinds. Wind whips,
whitewashes sound.
Words, stars, dark particles
spin into oblivion. Whole
towns. Entire centuries

carried along toward
a bend in the road,
the curve of the earth,
the turn beyond which
neither horse nor rider
nor light returns.

As Luck Would Have It

The guy didn't
get the girl

and she, in turn
didn't get pregnant

nor, after all,
did she get

the dream house
or runner-up.

He didn't get
very far ahead,

didn't get over her
for decades.

Neither of them
got rich or wise,

or what they
always wanted,

And like most of us,
they still don't get it.

Moon in Virgo: Analytical

Your analytical bent will keep you
from falling head over heels
for the next cowboy poet who kicks off
his boots in your bedroom—
all big teeth and thank-you-ma'am,
range and ranch and rodeo
till the cows come home. Sweeter
than heck, yes, but there's something
so borderline about a man
who pillow-talks in rhyme and meter.
You're cautious, meticulous, good
at sifting information, seeing clues—
like him whistling "Sweet Caroline"
a whiff of Ravished Rose on his collar.
Also, the collect call from Spokane
should've been a dead giveaway.
You've always been good with numbers
and when you add up two and two,
you come up with red lights, danger signs.
From now on, you won't fall for a tall
tale, take the bait, or swallow his line.
Your rising star is about to make
an appearance and you're planning
to be in the right place at the right time.

Moon in Virgo: Monsters

Today's advice is to let
the monster out of the closet,
engage it in conversation.
As if it only wants a good airing
like a musty fur coat
and will afterward slink off,
leaving you in peace. But,
not so fast and which monster?
The apprehensions, banes,
and dreads of a lifetime
are shooting craps in the back.
They smoke smelly cigars
and slam empty whiskey
glasses on the table.
They argue among themselves
and place bets on your demise.
In the dark, behind the coats,
panic crouches, wary, hooded.
Out of the farthest corner,
the cold and bony hand
of a long-buried secret
grips your wrist. And a small
army of niggling fears hides
in the toes of your shoes
plotting ambush and anarchy.

Disorderly Conduct

The glass slips. The milk spills.
Everyday objects succumb
to flux and flutter.

The apples have developed a mania
for the pears. They loll and roll
together, thick as thieves.

The stockpot boils over. Bowls
borrow trouble and bottles wobble.
Forks set up a clatter, stage
a ceremony of unrest.

In the closet, coats conspire
against the old order.
And my intractable shoes,
those sturdy little anarchists,
go their own way, leaving me
no choice but to follow.

Whaddya Say?

My ex is restless in the grave.
He always wanted to die
in a woman's arms, and I'm
glad they weren't mine.
He worried that the Afterlife
would be one never-ending
prayer party, crowds of angels
sucking on diet Sprites
and shouting *Amen.*

Maybe that's how it really is
because, even now, dead
and gone, he keeps turning up
at my door with his come-on
smile, his take-me-back eyes,
an open beer can sweating
in his hand. Sweetcakes,
he says, Sugarcube, Sassypants.
Whaddya say we live it up a little?

Cold Reading

I supply the words,
but you the meaning.

I provide the points,
you see them convening

in a pattern, a logical order,
a story emerging,

one you take up
without my urging.

I give what you need
to believe, to make sense.

My random breadcrumbs
you call evidence.

You remember the hits,
forget the misses,

forget my treachery,
remember my kisses.

Coffee With the Poet

This morning, I discovered
my favorite mug, abandoned
on a dusty bookshelf,
beside the collected works
of a poet with whom
I'd lately parted company,
he having left me craving
more of what I'd come
to expect, me having
finally admitted to myself
that things would never again
be the same between us.
In the beginning, it was all
"Dear Reader." He'd pull out
a chair, pour me a cup,
eager to share his latest
work. He had time, then,
to woo me, please me,
leave me breathless
and begging for more.
Later, he grew tired
of my attention, resented
my need for meaning.
Once, he said I bored him silly
and left me adrift mid-page.
Maybe that was the day
it became too painful
to go on. Maybe that
was when I sighed
in resignation, set down
my mug, and wandered
away to offer myself
to another rhyming liar.

My Whereabouts

My whereabouts
roam aimlessly.
They range and ramble,
drift, shiftless, sway, stray
far afield, wander
unwitnessed.

My whereabouts
wax whimsical,
dodge, hedge, dart,
and evade.

Cannot be pinned
with map tacks, trussed
with fast facts, assessed
with a death tax.

Cannot be charted
graphed, ambushed
unawares, caught
in your crosshairs.

Startled by My Reflection at Dusk

Afternoon draws its purse strings, turns
a cold shoulder. There's nothing left to buy
and even the windows are dark.

On the corner, some kids kick at the slush,
their laughter dull and metallic, as if
they already know what's coming.

Once, we thought the night was something
to own, something we could slip on,
disappear into. And then, we thought

we'd grow up to own it, to wear it
like a black velvet coat.

Accomplice

I'm the nondescript one in the heavy coat
and the black mood, pockets emptied
of keys and coins, water bottle confiscated.

I'm listening to the announcements, one delay
after another. It's the way we fly now, drained
and edgy, as if we haven't slept for a week.

At Security, an armed guard removes
a Makita drill from someone's duffel, waves it
like a weapon—which perhaps it is—

and scans the rest of us, all implicated.
We shrink into our suddenly insufficient skins,
avert our eyes and study our guilty hands.

I'm earbudded, buzzed with caffeine
and fluorescence, the one in the last row,
considering varieties of weather, whether
the flight will go, whether there's a code-word,
some inside information I should know.

.

Pointing the Finger

I blame the nightly news and the night nurse.
I blame barges and barrels and the burning bush,
the broken branch and the broken promise.

I blame the apparatus of weather, the mechanics
of wind and rain. I blame every fire and flood.
I blame the stubborn mountain, the endless plain.

I blame crumbling brick and rotting wood.
I blame dust and doubt and duty, the sense
of lurking danger and the certainty of pain.

I blame lost articles and lost causes. I blame
upper hands, the over-modified, the self-
satisfied, the stages of grief, the wages of sin.

I blame the double bind and the cherished illusion.
I blame the weak heart, the strong medicine.
I blame the mirror. I blame the skin.

Fleeting Thoughts

They slide away from you, slither,
slip, sand through your fingers,
a leaf trembling at the lip
of the falls, and then—

The sleek snake in dry grass,
nothing you can grasp,
too fast even for eye to claim.

Tail of a mouse that eludes
the broom, a nagging sense
that someone in the room
has called your name.

A flicker of form on the edge
of sight dissolving
into the scene behind it—
mantis, moth, chameleon.

The ace of diamonds shuffled
back into the deck, where only
a magician can find it.

The disappearing speck
of the flown crow high and away
against the clouds, heavy-
bellied, dull, and gray.

Sizing It Up

What fits is what
you get to live in—

a dependable dress,
worn jeans, things that cling
through thick and thin.

Serviceable ideas
and sturdy shoes, both
good for the long haul.

Face it. Longing
can eat you up, a hole
in the heart.

Love ravels, colors fade.
You were made
for greater things, still
waiting to come of age,
to swoon, to fall.

Yet age is what
you've come to, after all.

Your evil twin gets
to put on the Ritz.
You're stuck
with what fits.

A Brief History of Rain

Me standing in the rain and you
leaning close for our shoulders to touch,
the band screaming above the the storm.

Me standing in the rain and you
on your knees, slipping a paper ring
onto my wet and trembling finger.

Me standing in the rain and you
kicking the flat tire, regretting everything,
my feet held fast in the sucking mud.

Me standing in the rain and you
telling me how much we need it—
maybe the rain, maybe a break from it.

Me standing in the rain and you
expounding on cold fronts and pressure,
as if we were concerned with weather.

Me standing in the rain and you
watching from inside, a shadow
in the window, shaking your head.

Me standing in the rain and you
just a cipher, a name in the records.
You the absence that inhabits the rain.

Domesticity

The best way to cook rice is not
the best way to ask forgiveness.
That involves putting away the pots
and getting your knees dirty.

The best way to fold laundry is not
the best way to come to terms.
That involves the art of negotiation
and sometimes the art of war.

The best way to make the bed
is no way to restore harmony.
Only the foolish believe it, those
destined to lie awake, crying in the dark.

Despite what your mother told you,
housework has never solved anything.

Amusia

Since he was tone deaf,
she became a dial tone.
Defensive disconnection.

Once, she'd had musical
aspirations. Knew the bounds
of absolute and relative.

But every tune turned
into a one-note drone.
Perfect pitch to pitched battle.

She changed her tune
again and again
but he was not amused.

Aubade*

After Wendy Videlock

Nothing's more
annoying than

one   white

athletic sock

as if some hurried,
heedless jock

had fled your bed
with a badly put

adieu, anon—

and one bare
foot.

---

*This poem was inspired by, and follows the form of,
"There's Nothing More" by Wendy Videlock (*Poetry*,
January 2008).

Tango

We were always flying
apart or flung together

in a dangerous embrace.
Limbs bending to the force

of attraction, the pulse
of desire. Twin stars

locked in a death spiral,
afraid to answer

the unasked question.
Forever dancing around it.

When I Thought of Leaving

Our weedy lake, by then,
was murky with silt, clouded
with unasked questions
fishtailing through the shallows.
I scattered bits of bread
on the dusty surface,
watched for water snakes.
Like my own dark thoughts,
they coiled in the shadows
under the dock. The trees
leaned dangerously far
over the water, as if reaching
for a lover already gone.
I was hoping for something
sudden and priceless—
sun flashing on tail fin, a splash,
then waves rippling outward,
a black dog bounding
down the shore, a white bird
flapping free from its mouth.

Appliances

Most are in their teens now,
rebellious and unruly.

The toaster smokes
in the open, instead
of behind my back, tells me
to get over it, black is in.

The freezer's moody,
then manic, one day 20
below, the next 40 above.
The washer's off balance,
the dryer spins out of control.

Even the young ones,
asked to blend or grind,
grow fitful, whine and stall.
I humor them, check
for corrosion, frayed wires,
the source of the hum.

In their cool chrome
surfaces, I'm a woman
just getting by, waiting
for the next malfunction,

my placating smile
so distorted, it's hard
to say what I'll do next,
impossible to see
how much I love them.

Second Life

First, you must leave the one
you're in. Consider the little pill.
Or imagine the trance of the apple
under the spell of the knife.

It could begin with the slow glance
of a stranger, the way you're drawn
to danger, the way the flatline
of the horizon draws the eye.

It could begin with a slip of the wrist,
the twist, the cold grip of regret.
But the future's an untold story,
a book you haven't opened yet.

You still have time to think twice,
set your expectations higher.
You could be born again, become,
like anyone, an object of desire.

Recovery

When sense slipped
my grasp, I held on to air.

I listened to silence,
and called it language,

to the gabbling of geese
and called it providence.

I felt regret's whiplash
and called it justice.

I let mountains be doors
and rivers answers.

I waited to appear to myself,
willing to be undone

by a gust of grief
or irrational happiness.

Wayward

Left to my own devices,
I'm capable of staggering languor,

of shuffle and tarry
dawdle and delay.

Easily waylaid
by rambling rumination,

I formulate theories
of fortune and fancy,

scan the sky for signs
of magnificence

scan my face in the mirror
for signs of spring

I beguile myself
with ecstatic expectation,

woo myself with promises
of astonishment
all the wayward day.

How to Go

Go noiseless
on padded feet,

a curtain of dark
at your back.

Slip between shadows,
between trees.

Don't be afraid
to go hungry,

to leave questions
unanswered.

And like a lioness,
take everything

you love between
your teeth.

Imagine Me

The way I float the current
of your thoughts, take you swiftly
or by slow meander, the way
I can appear in any doorway
backlit by lamplight

the way I drop hints as casually
as articles of clothing, my easy
mouth full of red wine
and white lies, my arms open,
my agenda hidden

the way I lead you from question
to question, resist resolution
elude the obvious answer.
Imagine me one thing,
then another.

Dance Craze

Where I'm Calling From

I'm a little beyond the bend
of the river, a little up the road
from put together.

Out in the pasture of sweetgreen
where no one cares too much
for the upright or righteous.

The long haul is shorter
than it used to be, so much
magnificent light already spent,

every conversation more critical
than the last, each call more
susceptible to disconnection.

Tongues

I once loved a man who spoke in tongues,
who sang me rapturous
in the way of the river, in the way
of the waterfall, stunning the senses
with tingling light.

Above him, I was the mist that settled
into the valley at dawn. Beneath him,
I was the streambed, richly silted,
strewn with shining stones.

His language was a lesson in intention
and desire, a landscape where words
shrugged off the worldly, rose up
naked and true, gathered
into new constellations.

From him I learned the difference
between what is spoken and what is said,
learned that silence is a door that longs
to be opened, that any syllable
can be a lock. Or a key.

Secret

You hold it close
to your chest
like a hand
full of aces.

You could go places.
You're in the know.

All the time dying
to let it slip, you tip-

toe, zip-lipped,
through a minefield
of tease and wheedle

Dream of the sly
insinuation,
the careless innuendo.
The sweet release
of letting it show.

Any moment,
you could let it go--
a comet streaking

through space--
a brief glow interposed
between what's known
and only supposed.

We Fell

We tumble-rushed, toppled
topsy-turvy, headlong-over-heels

down the stairs of our excuses
down the well of our desires

needy and heedless
bound for the profound

down hills of hesitation
down the rabbit hole of doubt

stumble-spilled, slipped, slid,
lunged, plunged, plummeted

into one another's arms.

Wiring

We tore out old circuits,
fished new wires through the walls,

navigating by touch at night,
testing our footing, counting stairs.

Our hands slid along the walls, groped
for doorways, the edge of the bed,

the familiar gone strange, the old
house a new terrain of shifting sand.

The work done, we went on living
in the dark. We stumbled

from room to room, feeling our way
to temporary safety, reached out

for one another, grasping, giddy
as blindfolded children at a party.

Security Measures

My caution trips over itself,
a child in its father's shoes.

It drags me out of harm's way
straight into the path of disaster.

My caution builds fences
in all the wrong places—

between stepping stones,
between one day and the next.

It holidays in safety zones,
leaving me to feel my way in the dark,

to rest assured, or like a fool, to leap—
hoping a net will appear.

Storm Watch

The wind keeps us vigilant, but a blizzard
beguiles, then buries us.

The house leans into it, like a woman
who should know better, giving in
to disastrous love.

Once, we thrived on turbulence,
loved nothing more than a storm—
the little death wish of mutual consent.

Now, we scramble to batten and barricade,
navigate by lantern and shadow, hold on
to one another—

the air crackling with static, the taste
of mineral on the tongue.

Kitchen Two-Step

We aim for balance:
two bowls, two spoons, two hungers.
A small, simple meal.

A subtle art, this
pas de deux. Nimbly we step
around one another.

One deftly handles
the knife, while the other cries
over the onions.

We take turns checking
the pot, adjusting the flame
so nothing boils over.

One has an instinct
for how much pepper to add—
and is always right.

Sometimes, we glance up
and notice one another
smiling for no reason.

Across the kitchen
you're oh, so busy doing
your waggle dance.

This way to the nectar,
you signal. I follow your lead
straight to dessert.

Ode to the Ways of My Error

Here's to missteps and faux pas
and infelicities

to every slip and trip and fault,
to cherished fallacies

to steps in the wrong direction,
to screw-ups in judgment or action

to foulups and flubs and snafus
due to miscue or miscalculation

to blunders, bungles, and bloopers
to botches and snarls and jumbles

to boners and gaffes and lapses
and labyrinthine muddles

O klutzy flummox! O pratfall!
O stupendous clumsy stumble!

How varied, how myriad the ways
that serve to keep me humble.

Dance Craze

He worries constantly that I'll forget
which side of the bed I'm buttered on,
tripping over accidental accessories,
stumbling through claustral halls.
Even our best friends consider us
mismatched, one brown, serviceable
shoe, one sassy, strappy number,
cut out for dazzle and fancy footwork.

There's always something one can say
to gloss over missteps—like how about
that for a smooth maneuver? Like,
now you see it, now you don't. Like,
ho ho, now who's shoe's on the wrong foot?
It works every time. Everybody kicks back,
and takes to the floor, waiting to see
what the next dance craze will be.

We Ditzy Misfits

A fine kit and kaboodle we're in now,
my little piccalilli. Who but you
would have noticed the still pillow,
the spilled pills, spied the empty
bottle on the sill, so silly, so simple.
We two are a lucky-ducky duo: You,
my sane Jane. And I with no idea how
the jolly bottle got so unscrewed.
For now, let's call it an inexplicable
twist, an idiopathic slip of the wrist.
You get the gist. Come on, let's kiss.

The Forester's Wife

He wooed me in greenwood, beneath beech
and butternut, among fir and pine.

Sang of aspen and ash, dogwood, juniper,
yellowwood, and yew. His tune

the wind in spring leaves, hands rough as bark,
gentle as leaf-brush.

He showed me seedling, sapling, and shrub,
taught me to love the tender stem, budding branch.

At night he sighed his litany into my sleep—
sugar maple, sweetgum, truelove tree—

until it became the scaffold of my dreams,
the understory of our days.

And in the fall, the needles and nutshell,
the fleshy fruit, dark canopy overhead,
rustle of the forest night, its floor our bed.

Oh, heartwood, Oh, passion oak.
I whisper in his ear.
Oh, flame in the woods.

Promiscuous

> I'm greedy and restless, a little bit
> promiscuous with pronouns.*
>   – Cathy Park Hong

My I longs to consort with your I,
myself couple with yourself.

Let me take up with you, you conspire
with me, let's hobnob and accompany.

You and I could be we, couldn't we
mingle, mix, run around together

our limbs intertwine, your mine
with my mine, your this with my that.

Who knows which who and whose whom?
Let's connect, conjoin: Tempt fate, relate.

All the hours ours, ourselves united thus.
You and me, we. Objectively, us.

---

*The quote from Cathy Park Hong in the epigraph comes
from a conversation between Hong and Rachel Zucker on
the Commonplace Podcast, Episode 7, September, 2016.

Not as a Sheriff

On a line by Sandra Simonds*

The way I love you is not as a sheriff
who could round you up, lock you away
for safekeeping. The way I love you
is not as a preacher, ready with a sermon
or even forgiveness, and not
as a mechanic who could make things
run more smoothly. Not as a gardener,
a spray of blossoms in my hand
like a flimsy apology.

The way I love you is not as a rock.
I've never been that certain of anything.
And not as a house that can give you
shelter, a window that lets you look
in or out. The way I love you
is not as a road that knows where
it's going or what it's left behind.

I love you like a dream you've forgotten
we're in, a slash of light through trees,
rain drumming on corrugated tin. I love you
like an hourglass, a needle, a flame,
a whim to which you're suddenly inclined,
a taste of fruit, familiar but strange,
a tune you can't get out of your mind.

---

*From "Poetry is Stupid and I Want to Die," by Sandra
Simonds, *American Poetry Review*, Vol. 43, No. 5.

Phases

The moon's a study
in flux, a history of hello
and goodbye,

a lucky coin about to fall
into the slot of the horizon.

The rest is rumor—
madness and mania,
wolves at midnight,
seas and sonatas awash
in reflected light.

She'll always return,
throw off her borrowed veil,
come sweeping
to meet your need.

And you'll fall again
into her easy rhythm,
a ceremony of wax and wane
as waters rise and recede.

The Catch

My husband dreams of fish
making their way upstream.

I watch his eyes moving
under closed lids

as they scan the shallows,
follow the current

where wordless hungers
return to their source.

Moonlight ripples the sheets
and a shadow passes.

For thousands of nights,
I've studied his sleep,

a woman on the shore,
waiting to catch sight

of movement, a sudden
flash of iridescence,

a glimpse of silver fin,
the bright arc of its flight.

Relativity

Sometimes I think
I'm getting it—

how radios work
or why continents drift,
or why you can't step
in the same river twice—

Some inklings are slippery
as fish, some just flash
like light on water.

But once in awhile,
more than we can know
flickers on and off.

Like last night: the pull
of the current, land masses
shifting, the static
of distant stars—

me in relation to you
in relation to me.

I Was the Rain

I was the rain, always falling,
dropping delirious,
a cloudburst of complications.

I was mist, sprinkle, downpour.
drizzle and deluge,
flurry and flood.

I was cats-and-dogs
all over your countryside,

pattering on your roof,
sobbing at your window,

spoiler of picnics, ruiner of shoes,
mistress of mud and misery,

pooling, puddling,
pathetic, at your feet.

You were a dry spell, a desert
thirsty and yearning,
a refuge to run to, fall into.

I was the rain, and you
were two cupped hands.

Praise Poem

For the sunrise and the sunset of you
the gathering clouds, the sudden storm of you

the swaying to the blues of you
the talking to the birds of you

the silvering in the hair of you
the little bit of Neanderthal of you

the hazy shade of winter of you
the whiter shade of pale of you

the ghost in the machine of you
the tuneless shower repertoire of you

the winding river's way of you
the rolling wave and undertow of you

the comet's tail, the starry sky of you
the lit-up Eiffel Tower at night of you

the Iliad and the Odyssey of you
the Jack of Hearts, Jack of all trades of you

the abracadabra, the stitch in time of you
the sentimental valentine of you.

Siberia

A long season in a northern country—
whiteouts, impassable roads.

Under such conditions, who's to say
whose wrist cannot be twisted,
whose slit, whose hand holds the knife?

Snows pile up, banked like feather beds
and we slip into them, limbs moving
in slow motion, elderly angels
adrift in a downy field.

How I've Known You

The moment before thunder,
the relief after rain.

The striving in the furled leaf,
the fall of the last petal.

Ribbon of desire, the winding
path, illuminated.

The wave's swell and surge,
its crest and its breaking.

Breath and breathlessness,
my heart's patient visitor.

The question unasked
and unanswerable.

The shape of the thought,
the word before it finds my mouth.

Moving Like Fish in Moonlight

Come night, the river's fragrant
with wet grass and pine, the current

higher pitched, harboring hidden
logjams and cutbanks.

We soft-step the dark, slide into
the water, elude whirlpool and inlet,

and slow-stroke the inky stream.
We relinquish direction and desire,

all but the dream of fluidity,
to become a transient silver flicker,

an illusion of light as the moon's lamp
crests the dark and silent trees.

Riches

Sometimes the trees
breathed, and sometimes
they held their breath
while I listened to twilight.

Sometimes a searching hand
found mine in the dark
before I knew how much
I needed one to hold.

Often, the long wet
tongue of grace licked
my face joyous
as the found-again puppy.

Just once, the broken cup
leaped up from the floor
and reassembled
itself in my hand.
I drank from it.

Intimates

We have been intimate,
the past and I. I've swooned
over it like a drowsy
honeybee swollen with nectar
on a fruitful afternoon.

It suits me. Nothing's new,
though facts can be rearranged.
Sometimes names change
or slip away. Still, the light's
soft, voices muted.

The past's well suited
to my peace of mind, its spool
of memories easy to unwind,
A safety net, an ultra-cool
timeshare. Look for me there.

Be Mine, Valentine

My mindset's in fine fettle,
love, a joyful immoderation.
In spirits, prefers gin,
in weather, the whimsy of wind.
Let's ransack reason's
fusty cupboard and drink hearty.
Be mine, valentine, bring
me silly hearts and flowers.
The future's bleak, but ours.
Let's have us a party.

Heart Sounds

I listen to my heartbeat like a golden oldie.
I listen to my heartbeat, which seems to come and go.
I listen to my heartbeat, its own dark story.
I listen to my heartbeat and its undertow.

I listen to my heartbeat like distant thunder.
I listen to my heartbeat quicken, then slow.
I listen to my heartbeat, its murmur, its secrets.
I listen to my heartbeat and pretend I know.

Danube

To us, this long waltz,
a winding blue river,
clear and deep, that follows
a course we've memorized,
as natural as breath, as sleep.
We step and glide, guide
one another with a feather's
touch, a glance, a sigh.
To us, this slow dance,
its depths, its sweep. Turns
as practiced, smooth, and easy,
as the promises we keep.

About the Author

A long-time medical writer and editor, I've also taught creative writing in community colleges and adult education programs. I love the lively online poetry community and, for many years, have served as co-administrator of an online poetry forum, The Waters. I've published a poetry chapbook, *Smoke and Mirrors* (2013) and a full-length collection, *Chameleon Moon* (2014; reissued 2019). I live in Vermont, love French picnics, and play French café music on a sparkly purple accordion.

Mailing List

Let me know if you enjoyed these poems, or if you'd like to know when future books are published. Just send a note to antoniaclarkpoetry@gmail.com.

Join Me

On Goodreads or at antoniaclark.com.

Made in the USA
Monee, IL
23 February 2020

22192958R00059